The History of the Soul

The History of the Soul

including

Letters From People Who Remember Their Previous Lives,
or Certain Incidents Connected With the Past

by

Gervée Baronte

THE BOOK TREE
San Diego, California

Originally published
1930
E & F.N. Spon, Limited
London and New York
All Rights Reserved

ISBN 978-1-58509-324-3

New material & revisions
© by The Book Tree 2010

Cover layout
Atulya Berube
Toni Villalas

Published by
The Book Tree
P.O. Box 16476
San Diego, CA 92176
www.thebooktree.com

We provide fascinating and educational products to help awaken the public to new ideas and information that would not be available otherwise.
Call 1 (800) 700-8733 for our *FREE BOOK TREE CATALOG*.

Foreword

The author was a gifted psychic medium from England who was widely known in the early 20th century. Her main specialty was reading people's past lives and she developed a strong reputation for doing this accurately. Her books, like this one, often focused on reincarnation, the reality of the soul, what it really is, and how it works. She was totally and completely convinced in the cycles of reincarnation-how many of us have lived past lives, and will live again in the future.

This rare book would have disappeared had the publisher not found a copy and recognized it for its importance and spiritual wisdom. It answers such questions as:

How do we know that reincarnation is a fact?
Exactly why do we reincarnate?
What happens when the soul passes from this life into the next?
Under normal circumstances, how long does it take before we come back in another life?
Why do most of us not remember our past lives?

This book goes straight to the point and answers these questions clearly. It also includes a fascinating section of letters coming from people who remember their past lives, and often includes how they were able to verify them. These are amazing stories that leave little doubt as to the reality of past lives. The book closes with letters from those who acknowledge and appreciate the work of the author.

Paul Tice

Introduction.

RE-INCARNATION—THE HISTORY OF THE SOUL.

We study history because the knowledge of the past can be applied to our present needs. The present and the future have been moulded by the events of the past. Previous misfortune has taught us not to repeat the mistakes which caused it. Had we not profited by these previous mistakes each generation would be born into raw chaos. What we call civilization would never have been achieved.

*   *   *

Civilization is built on our past mistakes and the lessons we have learned from them. We are far in advance of the man who gnawed bones in a cave, but we are still that man. We have his passions, his desires, his endurance, his despair and his fear of the unknown. But we have learned to modify and to control these attributes.

*   *   *

If our material life has been improved by studying mundane history, how much more important it is to improve our spiritual life by studying the history of the soul. The soul (like our physical attributes) does not enter this life as a fresh creation. It comes from a long line of previous existences on this earth and elsewhere, during which progression it has acquired its inherent peculiarities. It has the strength and weaknesses of the temporal attributes. It also learns its lessons from mistakes in the past, and from these lessons it shapes its future destiny.

Re-incarnation is the history of the soul. It teaches us that the child opens each new existence with the characteristics derived from previous lives, and adds the experiences of a new personality to the sum total of the soul's traits. The essential self, or progressing ego, of an individual remains the permanent thread stringing together the separate existences. That we have forgotten the causes which produced the present sequence of pain, poverty, pleasure, talents, defects and failures is no disproof of them, and does not disturb the justice of the scheme. We know that the soul, while it is interested in material things, must find its happiness in the physical realms, and when its inclination is idealistic it will seek some expansion in the spiritual realms.

*   *   *

Granting the permanence of the spirit in every change, the doctrine of re-birth is the only one explaining the phenomenon of life. It is already accepted on the physical plane as evolution and is valuable in applying the law of justice to human experiences.

*   *   *

It is useless to try to explain the inequalities, miseries and injustices of life as the theologian does, by a future condition where men will be rewarded or punished for their deeds on earth. The theologian admits that God's earthly administration cannot be as good as His Government of some vague future state. The materialist, on the other hand, regards all the developments of life as the result of some blind natural force.

Science, the beloved Gospel of the materialist, is studying and classifying psychic facts. These investigations are bound to land science in the midst of non-physical facts and then it will be necessary to invent a new list of names (scientific names) for the psychic laws which Re-incarnation has always recognized.

There are several arguments in favour of Re-incarnation :

1. It explains immortality.
2. Science is steadily confirming it.
3. The progress of the soul demands it.
4. It answers the questions of reward and punishment.
5. It accounts for the injustice and the misery in the world.

*   *   *

The majority of human beings do not question the immortality of the soul, but they say that the soul is eternal on but one side of its earthly existence. Eternal means eternal. If the soul came into existence for this life only, why should it continue after this life is finished? It cannot be eternal unless it existed before this present life. The materialist, who believing that the soul originates with this life, declares that it ends with this life, is at least logical. A little reasoning shows us that that which originates as nothing must end as nothing.

If we believe in immortality we must admit that birth and death are but temporary shifts in the soul's progress. Whether the soul is a spark from some divine force or a cluster of separate energies, if we believe that it is eternal it must be indestructible.

The deduction is that it must have assumed many forms before it appeared in our present form. If we believe in the soul's continuance we must admit that birth is the death of a previous existence. Let us consider senile decay, or what is known as second childhood. Nature is showing us the condition of man's next life in depriving him of the memory of his life's experiences. This aged infancy shows that the conscious loss of life's details does not seem strange to nature.

*   *   *

On the other hand there are people who can remember from one life to another. Any number of people, when visiting places for the first time (in their present lives), feel that they have known the places before. Others can remember certain individuals whom they have known in a previous life. The Eastern records are full of cases of persons knowing some one they have met in this life because they remembered him as one they knew in the past. This is frequently the case with Indian and Burmese children who never heard of Re-incarnation. It is our memory of a previous enemy which causes us to dislike some one with no apparent reason. It is also the continuation of some former tie which makes us desert our homes and follow some one who has disturbed the even tenor of our present existence.

Karma, which is the doctrine of re-incarnation, is a Sanskrit word meaning action; but in re-incarnation this word is used to denote cause and effect. There is no sensible explanation of life but the scientific one that cause produces effect. Whatever debt we contract in one existence we pay in another. We should remember this when we complain of the limitations of our present lives.

We have shaped our own destiny. There is no Fate standing at the rudder of our lives. We are our own steersman. We suffer for our former mistakes and we are rewarded (by the progress of our own souls) for past virtues. This may seem unjust, because we ask, why should we suffer for what we cannot remember? We do not remember much about our present childhood if it comes to that, but if we make some serious mistake during our early years we suffer for it throughout our lives. If you fall down during childhood and break your leg you may limp all your life. This is the law of cause and effect in operation. "Divine justice" has nothing to do with it, for no Divinity would cause a child to break its leg.

*   *   *

Experimental evidence demonstrates that we actually forget nothing. All is stored in the soul memory, but the conscious mind has no recollection of the causes which have led to certain effects.

The History of the Soul.

FIRST CHAPTER

THERE has always been the quest for knowledge—always the desire to answer problems. Where have we come from? Were are we going? Why are we here? Every age has asked itself these questions, and all philosophies have been attempts to answer these questions. Thousands and thousands of books have been written about the eternal trio : birth, death and sex.

The early peoples erected gods on altars in the forests. These Gods were propitiated rather than worshipped. Early man made blood sacrifices before them and promised to perform feats of strength for them if they would listen to his plea and grant his requests. When famine or disease visited the country the gods were angry because they had not received sufficient sacrifices. Animals were slaughtered and dragged before them; the propitiators hoping that they would relent. The storm gods brought storm and destruction to appease their wrath by destroying property.

Whatever god we have erected whether it was the god of primitive man or the god worshipped by the religions of to-day, there has always been some form of propitiation. We have given our good works in the hope of future reward, thus taking out an insurance policy with eternity. Fear has driven us on, insisting that we " do right " if we hope for salvation. This " doing right " in order to achieve a position in one of the " many mansions " spoken of by Christ is a form of selfishness which a God of Love could not condone. We have accepted our sufferings and blamed God for visiting them upon us. Instead of trying to understand the law of evolution we have treated God as a pack-camel and burdened Him with all our troubles.

" Oh God let this burden be removed from my shoulders " is a prayer which will never be answered. We must know how to remove our own burdens.

All the suffering in the world we have produced ourselves. Our wars, diseases, famines, are all of our own manufacture. No suffering has ever been visited upon us by God. We are the victims of our own ignorance and we shall suffer until we contact the knowledge which will set us free. We have heard a lot about the faith that moves mountains. Faith is not necessary to move mountains. Mountains move themselves. Certain scientists know that several mountains have moved some distance since 1900. Mountains have always moved although we have but recently discovered this fact.

Evolution carries on whether we understand it or not. To understand evolution let us call it motion or vibration. Motion cannot cease for there is nothing but motion. We were put into the world by motion. Our bodies are nothing but forms of motion. When our essential-self leaves our bodies our bodies are switched unto another form of vibration. The cells of the body have their own form of life which manifests when the soul departs. The body may do nothing more than fertilize a plant but this is a form of continuity; the plant in turn generates other plants.

We produce rest by adding motion to motion consequently we cannot become absolutely still. We simply change our modes of motion. Sound, light, heat, electricity, magnetism, colour, are all one force to which we have given many names.

Evolution has paired its forms for balance, man and woman, mind and body, light and darkness, but these divisions belong to the same force. Everything we understand is a matter of sensation or vibration. Our sensations are under the law of our will. We can heighten them to receive joy, harmony and knowledge,—heighten them for anything which makes for advancement. We can refuse to harbour the sensations of sickness and sorrow; these sensations cause delay and consequently are unreasonable.

When we cannot work out a problem we do not sit beside it and weep. We study it until the light comes to us—until we see the answer. The problem we call death is but the working out of evolution. The law of advancement has many names. Each religion christens it according to its desires. Call it what you like, but it is nothing but motion in many forms.

The will can incline the mind in the direction in which it wishes revelation. The ego, knowing the desire of the mind, will contact the knowledge. The enlightenment may come in the terms of time and space. This is not because the knowledge is held in some future state, but because we cannot contact the vibration which would reveal our desires until we are attuned with a certain vibration. We are surrounded by forms of knowledge at every moment but we are not aware of this fact.

Sound transference is as old as the world but Marconi contacted the wave or vibration which revealed it. A person who contacts a portion of the surrounding knowledge we call a " discoverer." He has found nothing new, but he has become attuned to something. The fish does not know that he is surrounded by land. This is because his element is water and he can receive only the sensations of his element. This does not alter the fact that he is surrounded by land and other elements that he cannot understand. In the same way we are surrounded by many elements which we do not understand. We catch glimpses of them as the fish catches glimpses of the land. When great discoveries are made, such as Marconi's discovery, the discoverer is attuned to the surrounding knowledge. Everything in our human evolution is the result of desire becoming attuned to certain vibrations which can cause our desires to manifest. Our present world is the result of our former thinking, for everything we strongly desire meets its rate of vibration. We should remember this when we give vitality to worry, doubt and fear. Light and magnetism are rapid vibrations but thought is more rapid still. Human advancement or delay consists in raising or lowering our thoughts.

To cure disease we must heighten our sensations of health. Health is just as contagious as disease. We should think health. By thinking health we contact health, for the saying " we always get what we are looking for " is very true.

Our Western religions promise us eternal life for good works; but only if we live *after* death. We have lived before birth or the idea of eternal life is nonsensical. If we admit eternity then birth and death are relative terms. One must slope into the other continuously. Birth slopes into death, and death in its turn must again slope into birth, or the idea of eternal life is without foundation. We know it is not without foundation, for nature constantly " puts off the old man " before our eyes.

Many people have told me that the idea of re-incarnation takes all the joy out of life. They cannot bear the idea of constantly coming back here to suffer again and to learn further lessons.

If we direct our attention simply to the worship of God and close our eyes to everything in the universe we must wonder why a merciful tender loving father permits such suffering as we see about us. Granted that He is omnipotent and wise, why has He allowed the world to drift farther and farther into chaos. The only answer is that He is showing us that we are responsible for what happens in this world. He did not intend us to learn our lessons through suffering, but we have chosen to learn them by such means. We continuously practice destruction when construction is the law of evolution.

Re-incarnation is not a religion as many people think. It is a natural law in operation having to do with the carrying out of Nature's principles. It is no more religious than biology is religious. Without any consideration of theology, God's Laws operate in biology, and they operate also in re-incarnation. Re-incarnation is a truthful penetration into the laws of cause and effect which govern everything in the universe.

SECOND CHAPTER

TRACING CHARACTERISTICS.

EVOLVED souls carry a resemblance from one incarnation to another; such souls for example as Buddha and Saint Francis of Assisi. The love of animals, the receptivity to all impressions, the heroism and self-denial, the willingness (almost eagerness) to accept poverty were identical in these two great Saints. Another resemblance exists between Novalis and Raphael. The intellect of both these men is the same; their scientific mind, the approach to spirituality, their love of nature. I could go on indefinitely mentioning resemblances; but these already mentioned will suffice.

People write me about physical resemblances. They say they have the brow of some historical character, or the eyes of some famous person. One woman wrote that her profile was exactly the same as the profile of Beatrice Cenci; so she concluded that she must be the unfortunate Beatrice in another incarnation. We cannot trace the progress of the soul through physical resemblance; through soul-resemblance is the only way to trace the progress of the ego. The experiences the ego has in a certain body are stamped on the ego, not on the body it inhabits.

It is not necessary for the soul's development that the ego should live in two bodies which are exactly alike. Our past evolution up through the mineral, plant and animal kingdoms shows us that our ego did not inhabit two bodies of the same material. The ego must go on regardless of its vehicle. It attracts the vibratory wave, according to its knowledge, which decides its onward course. It inhabits the body on various planes of existence which its acquired knowledge has prepared it for. It can never halt in its progress. Its periods of rest are concerned with its progress; for, during its rest, it examines the knowledge it has acquired and prepares for its next journey. It is like a man who starts out on a long journey. He may travel on a boat, a train, a tram, an aeroplane, but *he* does not change in any of these vehicles. It is not necessary that the vehicles resemble each other. The man's idea is to complete his journey. He is not allowed to sail on a luxury boat simply because he behaved well on the train. No one waits at the various stations to punish or to reward him. He gained knowledge during his journey through his observations and his mistakes; and he chose the most comfortable means of transport according to his knowledge and to his means. The ego, heedless of material means, travels according to its knowledge.

The ancient Hindus believed that there is a permanent physical atom in every body; this atom, according to old writings, receives vibrations from the outside through the medium of its physical wrapping. It in turn repeats vibrations caused by the force of the outside impact. All the results of physical experience are said to be stored in this permanent atom.

The German embryologists had something like this Hindu belief in their minds when they taught physical heredity. They brought forward an idea something on the order of the Hindu teaching, to explain why a man reproduced the features of an ancestor. The Hindus believed that during the transition we call death, this permanent atom remains in the world. In other words, it stands to represent the life which has left it, the continuing ego. All the other atoms of the body leave it, bent upon their own work. It alone remains, because it alone retains all the experiences of the body it lately occupied. In a cocoon-like wrapping it sleeps during the years the Jivatma (spirit) is living in other worlds. When the time comes for re-incarnation, this is known by the vibration sent from the spirit in the other worlds to the permanent atom, which sends out a vibration for new body material; which material, attuned to the permanent atom, gravitates to it. The forces governing the atom see to it that it is reborn under the star which corresponds to its former experience. Consequently it is not the star that imposes the temperament, but the atom which has chosen the star. The atom then impresses all its past peculiarities on its new body.

This is a very elaborate structure to support the belief in individual re-incarnation. The structure breaks down, however, under the weight of a little reasoning. The evolutionary scheme of the universe is advancement. The continuing ego is constantly obtaining knowledge. The higher the knowledge, the higher the vibratory waves which it contacts. The ego must take the body which suits its rate of vibration. The egos which attract a lower vibratory wave do not attract a higher wave, consequently the waves which would energize the egos of one evolutionary plane would not quicken the egos of another. This rule holds with atoms (providing one could accept the idea of the permanent atom) as well as with egos.

We pay for our mistakes and evil doings with unhappiness, but while we pay with unhappiness we add to our store of knowledge.

Our human body is on a higher plane of evolution than the bodies of other animals and of plants; but we are all on the same thread—the thread of life.

Worship of any sort raises our vibrations. Next to knowledge it attracts the highest vibrations, for it generates love. But knowledge, being the key to advancement, must be put before love.

We often hear people talking about the lower forms of life. There is no low form of life any more than there is a high form. Life is life. Man is capable of responding to the lowest as well as to the highest vibrations. The capacity does not necessitate the *desire* to respond. There is neither right nor wrong in the eternal scheme of things. There is wisdom and ignorance. The divine essence wills to express itself through evolution; knowledge. It is the divine essence in everything which wills for expression Everything desires to break out of its prison. The chick breaks through the shell, the seed breaks through the ground. Our soul (ego) breaks through the flesh. Our body may fear what we call death, but our ego is ever willing its self-expression. The life (divine) essence must express itself by change.

In spite of the souls' desire for freedom it is well to live in a body as long as we can, for we are constantly adding to our knowledge while we occupy the flesh. The Christian West has made up its mind that we shall live for three score years and ten. All the Western races believe this, consequently the people of the West pass on at the age of seventy. As I have said in another chapter, we usually get what we seek for we contact the vibration which produces it. The people of the East, knowing nothing about the Christian Bible or the belief in three score years and ten, often live to be well over a hundred. I employed a washerman when I lived in China who was a hundred and six (his age reckoned by our calendar) and I am sure he would have resented it if I had told him that he had outlived his allotted time.

The stage known as senile decay is reached earlier in the West than it is in the East. Passing from old age into childhood is exactly what the ego does at the end of the earthly cycle. Senile decay is the forerunner of the change which takes place when we have completed one incarnation and are ready for another. When the soul rests in the intermediate realms it does not take on the character of a child; but there is no way for it to be reborn on this planet without fulfilling the law of this planet. We enter a child's body at rebirth, but our soul-memory remains intact.

Many children are much older than their parents, or even their grandparents. Age is concerned with the soul, not with the body. A child prodigy is a soul which reached a high rate of development in one line in a previous existence. Mozart disproves all the hazy ideas about genius, for he *remembered* the operas without being taught to play them. Genius could not account for the fact that he played every note correctly when he was but five and six years of age.

Science tells us that a genius is one whose mind has developed along one line to the detriment of all other lines. This is just one more statement which means nothing. Science forgets to tell us where and how the mind developed along one line. When I was in New York a few years ago I heard a famous American Scientist say that genius was caused by decayed tissue. Of all the explanations of genius I think this the most absurd. It means that one needs only to let his brain atrophy if he would become a genius. I have known many people who through laziness and indifference have allowed their brains to become slack, but I have never found a genius among them.

THIRD CHAPTER

Cosmic Communications.

The faculty known as intuition is often nothing more than telepathy. One ego is communicating with another. In transference of thought the will may or may not be called into play. When the soul seeks the cosmic realms, where it rests between the incarnations, it carries its memory with it.

Strange and unusual thoughts often come to us from egos dwelling on the cosmic plane. I do not refer to what is known as " spirit messages," but to thoughts in our own consciousness which we cannot understand. I fail to see how a departed ego who is on another vibration can return to earth unless it comes to re-incarnate in another body; which would enable it to use this vibration. If a departed ego communicates with this vibration (and I am not saying that it is impossible) it could not return to earth to " deliver messages." It could communicate from its own realm on vibratory waves, for everything in this universe, and in the intermediate states where the soul rests, depends upon vibration.

Each soul is a receiving station like a radio machine, and we receive long and short vibrations as the radio instrument receives long and short waves. All impressions reach us from *without* on vibratory waves which penetrate matter. The human eye responds only to those vibrations which produce the sensation called light. It is capable only of discerning objects which can issue or reflect light according to its vibratory response. Our ears respond only to those exceedingly slow vibrations which affect the air surrounding us. There is an infinity of light waves too swift to be perceived, and millions of sound waves too fast or two slow to register on the human ear. The vibrations which, so far, we see and hear are scarcely worth mentioning in the vast range of light and sound. The communications of a departed ego would be restricted to those vibratory waves which could penetrate earthly matter.

During what is known as the dream state, a departed ego would be more apt to communicate with an ego dwelling on the earth for the conscious mind of the earth—dweller—the mind of opposition—would be quiescent and the essential-self (that which continues) would be better able to receive the message.

With advanced egos, dwelling on the earth, the *will* to receive communications may be called into play. This is done by becoming susceptible to higher vibrations. Egos who can wilfully become susceptible may keep up a constant exchange of thoughts with egos on other vibrations.

All through the ages we have been taught that everything comes from within. "Look within" we are constantly told by teachers of theology. A little thought will disclose the fact that nothing comes from within. We cannot take out of a soul (a continuing ego if you prefer) something which has not already been put into it. The

Divine voice within is nothing more nor less than the experience the soul has acquired during its earthly and non-earthly journeys. Imagination, which many people think is some " such stuff as dreams are made of " is simply the faculty of mixing some old knowledge with an idea which *strikes* us. It is nonsense to think that we could take something out of our mind which was not already there. When an idea strikes us, we are contacting some vibratory wave which has aroused our soul-memory.

Everything in this universe is a matter of contact. This makes susceptibility the keynote of life. How much can we become susceptible to and use. Christ told us to " resist not evil." He did not mean that we should seek evil, but that we should learn from it. Whatever lesson our soul needs it gets whether we learn it from what is known as evil or what is known as good.

Clairvoyance and clairaudience come naturally to persons who can extend their susceptibility. It is not a question of vision or of hearing, but of the power wilfully to become susceptible. There is nothing superhuman in such susceptibility. Some day the entire mass will catch up with the clairvoyant. What the clairvoyant contacts is nothing distinct in substance from that which is surrounding all of us. Everything is in motion. There is slow and there is rapid motion governed by the power which it contacts. The higher rates of vibration are reached by knowing how to contact them. The average person finds them impeded by the flesh. Just as certain batteries are attuned to slight voltage, our flesh is attuned to slight voltage of the higher cosmic forces. If a strong current were to enter a battery which was not attuned to it, it would shatter the battery. In the same way a powerful current from the higher cosmic forces would shatter the average body.

We would not be conscious of our bodies were it not for the energy which flows into our flesh. When this energy leaves us we are no longer conscious because this *outside* energy constitutes our life.

If we could be isolated from all the world's turmoil and allowed to extend our susceptibility, we would be able to contact the higher vibrations. As this is impossible and as we are surrounded by the world's affairs we can catch only an occasional glimpse of that which vibrates to the higher forces, and then only when our senses are momentarily attuned; for example in flashes of that which we call intuition. The world, misunderstanding this, looks with suspicion upon the man or woman to whom these flashes are revealed. The clairvoyant, who is supposed to give some sort of message, or disappoint his public, is inclined to distort his vision by trying to bring it down to physical comprehension. It does not follow that he has not seen clearly, but, owing to the difference in the vibratory rates he cannot describe what he has seen. I am speaking now of the clairvoyant who can extend his vision to the higher vibrations. The clairvoyant who talks of personal things is tapping the sub-conscious, or deeper thought, of his client. The hysterical psychism which is frequently met with is due to allowing the sympathetic (or nervous system) to control the brain. One who sees a vision at the expense of his physical body is not clairvoyant. He is the victim of some weakness which has for the moment broken down all physical barriers. True clairvoyance does not weaken the health by heightening the faculties.

Many clairvoyants can describe what is happening in an adjoining room. There is nothing remarkable about this. The clairvoyant has simply contacted one of the penetrating waves. We use some of these lower waves now with the help of machinery. The machine is not the wave; it is the substance through which the wave passes. If the human eye is in harmony with the wave, it takes the place of the machine. All this is a physical law in operation. There is nothing opaque in the universe. We call things opaque which our vision has not as yet penetrated. The so-called opaque bodies are those not capable of reflecting light waves with which we can vibrate. Any wave that can penetrate through walls can expose objects at a distance. There is no more danger of these waves becoming tangled than there is of the vibrations of light becoming tangled. A clairvoyant who can contact a wave which passes through a wall can follow that wave any distance by extending his vision. I often do this to trace objects for my clients. Anyone possessing concentration can learn to do this. It means simply to contact the lower rates of vibration.

All thought takes form in space and contacts its rate of vibration. Voice creates a greater disturbance in space and therefore is more powerful than thought. All statements with force behind them produce an effect. This is the secret of magic. Magic formulae is usually chanted. It has very definite rhythm. The student sending out a thought can produce an effect just so long as he can energize his thought-form. When his mind wavers his thought-form breaks up. The real occultist knows that self-control is but the first step on his pathway. He must acquire force-control if he hopes to understand cosmic communication.

FOURTH CHAPTER

Remembering Past Lives.

Many people, with whom I have discussed the immortality of the soul, have said, "If we have lived before, why cannot we remember anything of our past lives?" This statement implies that because the one making the statement cannot recall anything of his past life, it precludes the fact that anyone can remember his past life. It is the same as saying, because I cannot play the violin no one can play it. Few people can recall the incidents of their childhood; but no one would deny that he existed as a child. It is also true that many people cannot remember from one year to the other just what has happened; and we all know people, who, if they put anything down cannot recall where they left it.

But there are people who *can* remember their past "lives." In India, where the belief in re-incarnation dates back to the early Hindu civilizations, many people can recall their past existences. Certain ones can recall their entire "life" in a previous existence; others remember incidents. One explanation of this is that prejudice need not be fought. A Western person, remembering anything of his past life, would hesitate to mention it, because people who do not believe in re-incarnation would think he was drawing on his imagination. People are always ready to condemn what they know nothing about. A man told me not long ago that he did not believe in the science of occultism, and that he considered anyone who did, quite " potty." When I asked him if he knew anything about occultism he had to admit that he knew nothing, and had read no books on the subject. In most cases I find this is true of people who do not believe in re-incarnation. They know nothing about it. It would be quite useless to tell them that it was one of the tenets of early Christianity, and that the study of Nature proves it. They have *decided* not to believe and there the matter ends. I have also been told, when mentioning my investigations in India, that the Indians believe in re-incarnation because their religion teaches them to believe. I might say that the people of the West disbelieve re-incarnation because their religion has taught them to disbelieve. It is true that prejudice delays the receipt of a lot of knowledge which we could easily contact with an open mind. During my travels in India with various people, I met a man who described the town of Budd Gyha (the place where Buddha received his enlightenment) without having seen the place (in his present incarnation) or having read anything about it. He described the inside of the large Buddhist temple even to the number of shrines around the walls. He mentioned the figures which were on the shrines, and a flight of burnt-brick stairs which led to one of the figures. When I visited Budd Gyha later with him and a party of friends, we failed to find the shrines which he described, or the stairs leading to one of the figures. He simply shrugged his shoulders and said: " I always had the impression that the temple was as I described it; but I have no idea why I should have had such an impression." Several days later one of the party found an ancient record *written in Sanskrit* describing the temple as this man had described it. When we told him about it he went to no end of trouble to invent some reason for his impression *not* bearing on re-incarnation. When asked how he could have known about it considering that the old record had never been translated, he became quite disturbed, and accused us of trying to force upon him the belief in re-incarnation. When we asked him why he gave us a description of the town as it was in Buddha's day (another ancient record agreed with his description) he became quite angry and started a useless argument about pre-existence which got us no-where. He is an example of the prejudiced mind. With an open mind, and the willingness to investigate, we may find quite a number of people who can remember something, if not all, of a previous existence. I have questioned hundreds of people in various parts of the world regarding their recollections of previous lives. I have obtained a large amount of material; some of it in the form of intimate confessions which I have been asked not to mention for fear that others might consider the confessors " rather queer." Needless to say it has been Western people who have asked me to keep their secrets. My Western investigations have not always met with this desire for secrecy however. When I was writing about re-incarnation for *" Pearson's Weekly,"* I asked through that magazine for any evidence which my readers could produce of re-birth. The response was most gratifying. I received several thousand letters from people who could recall incidents in the past. Some of these letters I shall quote at the end of this chapter. In certain cases the evidence seems very clear. Other letters are vague and shadowy; but to a student of re-incarnation they point to the " carry-over " of the essential or soul-memory. I have reconstructed the past lives of some of my correspondents and found that they had lived in the places they were describing. I am always gratified, if my Hermetic Symbols, when they are set up and studied, reveal the " life " which my client remembers. The symbols do not always reveal what a client *feels*; although they are usually correct if there is some way in which the case can be investigated. Not long ago I received a letter from a client who said that she could remember having been stabbed to death in Rome. I put her symbols up and studied them from every angle, but, while I traced her through the Roman existence, I could find nothing to indicate that she had been stabbed. I found her passing out of the Roman existence quite peacefully. I concluded that she must have experienced the stabbing in some dream which was so vivid that she felt she had actually lived through the experience. There are people who would say that " astral flight " explained the stabbing, and that my client had been stabbed astrally. This explanation seems utter nonsense to me. I admit that the ego, soul, essential-self, whatever one wishes to call it, can travel regardless of the flesh, but I cannot admit that a non-physical thing can be stabbed.

As I have mentioned in another chapter, if the ego did not leave the body, the conditions known as sleep and as unconsciousness would not be possible. Material scientists who usually proceed by disproving one " fact " in order to prove another, say that sleep is caused by certain fluids in the body slowing down and producing fatigue. Very well; but we can experience the worst sort of fatigue without sleeping. If sleep is simply a matter of fatigue, why do we frequently find it impossible to sleep when we are suffering from utter exhaustion. Many people can arrive at the state of unconsciousness, known as sleep, by exerting their will. This does not look much like fatigue.

In the state of self-hypnotism, known as trance, physical unconsciousness can be produced by auto-suggestion. This has nothing to do with fatigue.

The memory of everything we have experienced is stored somewhere in the soul-memory. Persons who have barely escaped drowning have told how their entire life was *shown* to them in that brief moment when they hovered between life and death. As the soul passes from one vibration to another the entire " life " which the soul is leaving is flashed from the sub-conscious, or soul memory, into the conscious mind. Doctors tell us that most people are unconscious at the time of passing. In a way they are right because the soul has gone so far into the new vibration that it is almost unconscious of the vibration it is leaving. But there is a moment between the vibrations when the entire experience of the passing vibrations is flashed to the coming vibration. In this moment when the soul makes its supreme effort, the entire " life " of a soul is sometimes seen. In other words, people who have switched back into this vibration when they had *almost* entered the next realm, have told us how they saw the entire sequence of their existences in that moment of revelation. A man who was resuscitated after apparent drowning told me that he saw the panorama of his soul's wanderings in that moment between two spheres. He saw himself in China, India, Egypt and living with a primitive tribe in Africa. When questioned as to how he knew himself in these various aspects, he said he didn't know *how*, but he knew that he was the Chinese, the Indian, the Egyptian and the African he was watching.

Students of re-incarnation know that the soul is not interested in the body it uses if it gains the experience it seeks. During its journey it inhabits many bodies and uses many personalities, but the essential part of it—that which continues does not change.

I have been asked why it is that so many people who want to believe in re-incarnation, think they were kings and queens in previous lives. We must go into the realms of psychology to explain this. It represents a device upon which to rest an inferiority complex. Certain people who must occupy what they consider a humble position in this life, get a sort of satisfaction in thinking they were important people in some previous existence. In my investigations I have met hundreds of Cleopatras, Mark Antonys, Napoleons and Joan of Arcs. This happens in Western countries, for I have met in India and China, people who thought they had been slaves and brigands. One woman went so far as to tell me that only kings and queens and important people re-incarnated—that slaves and servants went to some vague limbo she could not describe. Another question with which I am often confronted is, " If we progress *why* should a previous king be a servant or a shopwalker in this existence? " I fail to understand why a soul has progressed because it has worn the body of a king or queen. The soul is not concerned with worldly positions. Who would say that the soul of Henry the VIII had progressed very far? The soul of many a servant or shopwalker has made greater progress. The soul may progress much faster in a humble position than it can in an important one. The soul of Henry the VIII progressed to the worldly position of king, but because of karmic debts contracted in that incarnation, his soul returned to a body where it could learn its lessons through physical suffering, such as it had inflicted upon others.

I do not wish to mislead you when I say the fundamental

part of us does not change. There is a difference between the surviving spirit—called in old writings the over-soul—and the ego or essential self of us. The eternal spirit dwells in everything but we have been given a will and the opportunity to achieve perfection by our own struggles. The soul of a king can inhabit the body of a servant to learn the lessons necessary for its progress, but this has nothing to do with people who would give themselves importance or gratify their self-esteem by saying they were kings and queens in past incarnations.

Children often remember their past existences, but because they meet with discouragement, or fun is made of them, they dislike to mention what is in their minds. Very soon their daily lives, and the prejudice of their elders, crowd out the psychic attribute which every child has at birth, until they themselves can laugh at what formerly seemed so real to them. If we listened sympathetically to what a child says it *feels* about things, we might learn something of the psychic or hidden side of life. This must be done while a child is very young—before it is seven—for as it swings farther into its new vibration it loses touch with the old.

In India it is not uncommon to hear a child talking of its previous existence. Those of you who have read my book " *You Have Lived Before* " will remember the Indian child of nine who insisted that she was the wife of a Mohammedan living in another village. Her Hindu family finally took her to the village she mentioned and found the Mohammedan whom she said had been her husband. He was questioned and admitted that his wife had passed on about twenty years before the interview which was then taking place. The child told him the name of his wife and related many incidents of their married life. She was correct in every statement.

There is a village in Burmah where children are questioned when they are old enough to talk about their condition in their previous lives. In many cases they can remember and they tell a connected story of their previous existences. They have been known to tell their previous names, which, on investigation were found to be correct.

As our days follow each other the impressions made upon the soul by our daily lives are filed away in our memory, but are apparently obliterated in our waking consciousness. Were this not so we would become insane from the pressure of all these various impressions. The memory of every detail of our childhood could add nothing to further our adult progress. But our past records can be opened by association of ideas or by being confronted with some scene of our childhood. In the same way people whose memory goes beyond their present existence can recall some incident of a pervious life when confronted with the scene of their past existence.

When the soul-memory is unusually clear it is not necessary for some incident to arouse it; for I have known of people remembering their lives in Egypt, of the early Dynasties, when they have never (in their present existence) visited Egypt.

I am asked occasionally, " What is the cycle of re-incarnation? " This varies according to the progress of the soul. Some people re-incarnate almost at once. Others spend hundreds of years between births. The average cycle (if we can say there is an average) is from one hundred to one hundred and ten years. People who pass out in violent disturbances, such as wars, floods and earthquakes, are apt to re-incarnate within a short time. In making the reconstructions of my clients' previous lives, I find a number of young men and boys who passed out in the world war.

People who can remember buildings which are about one hundred or two hundred years old can reconstruct the period in which they lived. Such a case occured when I travelled with a friend in Sicily. She described a house in every detail about a week before we visited it. She had never been in Sicily before, but she knew the house she was describing was somewhere on the Island. When we discovered the house (she recognised it by the exterior) we were told by the people who occupied it that it had looked just as my friend described it about a hundred years previously—"during grandfather's time." Even the pictures my friend had described hung on the walls " in grandfather's time." This placed my friend's former incarnation in Sicily about a hundred years before we visited the old house. Her memory of the house intrigued me and I reconstructed her former life with my symbols. I found that she had lived in Sicily, that she had never married, and that she had devoted her life to the care of her brother's invalid wife. Inquiry disclosed the fact that " grandfather's sister " had taken care of " grandmother." Her life had been a sort of sacrifice to an invalid and to her brother's children. My friend had been quite young when she passed from her Sicilian incarnation. The family told us that " grandfather's sister " was twenty-five years of age when she *died*. They admitted never having seen her.

LETTERS FROM PEOPLE WHO REMEMBER THEIR PREVIOUS LIVES, OR CERTAIN INCIDENTS CONNECTED WITH THE PAST

LETTERS

The following letters have been received by me at various times since I have been residing in England. I use the initials of my correspondents; but if any of my readers are interested in meeting the writers of these letters I shall be pleased (after obtaining permission from the writers) to furnish them with names and addresses. The second letter in the series is an exception, as the writer has already asked me not to mention her name.

I would call your attention to the last letter of the series. The " recurring dream " this correspondent describes is a very clear case of soul-memory operating when the conscious mind was in abeyance.

No word of these letters has been changed. I give them as they were received.

G.B.

*   *   *

First Letter.

When in practice as a Bailiff, I had in my employ a Possession Man, we nicknamed " The Duke " because of his lordly airs, and obviously superior breeding.

I left him one day " In Possession " at an old Manor House; when I called the next day, he was strangely excited, and told me with obvious conviction, that he was sure he had lived there before—as master.

He told me how he had found his way about the rambling old place without effort, that he had been sure, before he opened any of the numerous doors, exactly what sort of room it led to.

Although I ridiculed his idea, I could not but be impressed, he was so sure about everything. Then he gave the tenant and myself startling proof of his foreknowledge of the place. " There was a duel in this room " he said,— " and the victim of it was buried in the garden "; he showed us the spot, and begged us to dig.

More to satisfy the old man than in the hope of finding anything, we did, feeling rather foolish all the time,—we found bones—afterwards proved to be those of a man—a steel buckle, and a sword of the Cromwell period.

I was able to procure the sword for the old man who insisted it was his own.

B.H.

Dear Miss Baronte,—You may consider the two following incidents rather striking; but unfortunately, I cannot give the name or address for publication, as it is that of a great friend; and I know she would not like it.

I could give it to you provided that you would, as I say, not publish it.

My friend has a son who, as a small boy, was very different to the others. His parents looked upon him as highly imaginative.

(1)

They went to Ireland, and the boy had never been there; yet, on arrival, he proposed to his father that they should go down to the sea.

The father said " Well! Wait a bit my boy : we've only just arrived, and we don't know the way yet." The boy replied " Oh yes! It's down that path, through a gate-way with a lot of Latin writing on it." On investigation, this was found to be correct : a gateway, with a long Latin inscription. None of the family had ever been there before.

(2)

When the Dorking Motor-road was made, the boy, going along it for the first time, said to his mother, " There used to be a church at that corner, and I played the organ in it, and there were a lot of men with long gowns, and staves in their hands, and oyster-shells in their hats." The mother thought him, as usual, imaginative; but she was startled later, when looking up some old records, she found that a church *did* stand there, on the pilgrim-road to Canterbury; and was frequented by the pilgrims for Mass on their journey.

O.A.

Third Letter.

Dear Miss Baronté,—In writing this to you, I am in doubt as to it being direct evidence of re-incarnation. I leave that for you, who understand these things better than I, to judge.

All my life I have been haunted by a re-occuring dream, my earliest clear recollection of it being when I was four years old. I dream of going down steps into a cellar and walking along a passage. After I have gone a short distance it seems that the roof suddenly presses on me, I sweat and groan as I try to reach the light I can see in the distance, but I never manage to get out, almost always I wake up in an agony of fear.

When I was thirteen I went to stay with a school chum at a little village just outside Peterborough. It was during the war and quite a lot of houses were standing empty, one of which was a farmhouse. This house fascinated me, and I got my chum to go inside with me to explore.

She was scared, said the place had been empty years and was supposed to be haunted; I, on the other hand, felt strangely at home which was odd as I was a rather nervous child.

When we got to the kitchen I felt that something was wrong and began to look round. I must have looked puzzled for my companion asked me what was the matter and what I was looking for. " The cellar doorway," I replied as much to my own surprise as hers. Telling me not to be silly, there was not any cellar, she pulled me outside.

That evening we told her granny, a lady of ninety who was really great granny to my chum, where we had been, and about me looking for a cellar door. I don't think I was really surprised, when, looking at me very strangely she told us that years ago when she had been a very young woman there had been cellars, but one day the roof of one had caved in and despite the desperate efforts of the farmer, the couple's only daughter had been killed by the falling masonry. The couple, very much upset, had blocked up the remaining cellars and bricked in the opening. Since this my dream has been less frequent, coming usually when I am in poor health. I wonder if I really was killed in that cellar.

Yours very truly,

G.R.C.

*   *   *

FOURTH LETTER.

I was born in the Midlands and when a boy of 12 years was taken by my parents to the seaside; to be exact, a day-trip to Mumbles Head, South Wales. I was delighted with my first view of the sea, but a little puzzled that everything seemed familiar.

As we strolled along the shore under the cliffs, my mother remarked that she was very tired and " simply dying for a cup of tea." My father said it was a long way back to any place of refreshment but I insisted that a little further on, just round the headland, we could climb the cliffs by means of a rough path and would find a cottage standing a short distance back from the edge. Though my father pooh-poohed the idea and asked me jokingly if I could see round corners, my mother said that no harm would be done by going that far, and sure enough I led them to the path. We climbed the cliffs, and there a little way inland was the cottage.

Whilst waiting for our meal in an old-world room I knew the place thoroughly—every article of furniture, that old fashioned fireplace, everything; but had never been out of the Midlands before. I must have been a very determined youngster for I insisted on familiarity with my surroundngs and at last, as proof, said that I remembered a knot hole in one of the window shutters through which a beam of light used to cut across the room when they were closed in the early morning. To humour me, my father took me outside and asked me to find the hole. The shutters had not been used for years and were overgrown with ivy, but on holding a portion aside, there was the knot- hole.

This caused my parents to cease teasing me concerning my belief that I had been there before, and on the return railway journey the conversation turned to re-incarnation.

This was my first " proof " that I have lived before— a conviction that has lasted throughout my life and been strengthened by other incidents.

G.C.

Fifth Letter.

Dear Sir or Madam,—While serving as a Private Soldier in the Royal Garrison, Artillery, British Army, Regt. No. 1421317. On our way to China on the troopship s.s. *Delta,* P.&O. Line, 1921. The troopship docked at the Port of Bombay for eight hours. Myself and my chum, Gunner Jones, got permission to go ashore for a few hours. Although I had never been in Bombay before, it seemed to me as we walked from one street or Avenue to another, looking in the shop windows, that I had a feeling that I seemed to know what streets to walk on, and had a feeling or knowledge that I had been in this City of Bombay before.

As it was a very hot day, we went into a tea room and sat at one of the little tables. An Indian waiter came to take our order, he looked at me, there was a queer feeling came over me, and I spoke to him, but to the amazement of my chum, I did not speak in English but in the Hindustani language. The conversation lasted about a quarter of an hour to the amazement of the Indian Waiter who told me and my chum that he did not know that a whiteman could speak fluent Hindustani like I did. After we left the shop my chum kept asking me questions, such as, " I did not know you could speak the Hindustani language. Where did you learn to speak it? Have you been in India? before? "

My answer to my chum's questions was, I have never been in India until that day, I did not learn or was not taught to speak Hindustani and I did not know I could speak it. I was even surprised and worried myself over this.

J.H.E.

Sixth Letter.

Re-incarnation.

I was born in a village on the seacoast of Cornwall close to where a large Spanish Galleon was cast ashore during the breakup of the Spanish Armada.

It was probably from a survivor of this vessel that my family and myself derived the black hair, olive complexion and general appearance which seemed to speak of something Spanish in the way of an ancestor.

I was 25 years of age, and just recovering from a severe illness when I had a vivid dream. I saw myself, dressed in a light Spanish armour, digging feverishly in a hollow of a seacave some three miles from my home in which I had played countless times as a boy. I saw myself finish digging, place something in the hole, cover it with big loose rocks and then run away as fast as the uneven ground would allow.

The following night I again had an exactly similar vision, but as it did not recur, the incident was partly forgotten. Curiously enough, exactly twelve months afterwards, I had the identical dream again, and as I was not working, and knew the exact spot indicated in my dream, I decided to go and investigate.

Reaching the cave at low water, I just managed to scramble in, and was very busy indeed for the next four hours moving some uncommonly heavy lumps of rock. My dreams had been so impressive that I felt very little surprise to find, under the last rock, a box of copper with brass strips and hinges. This contained money and valuables, and the latter proved to be worth many times their intrinsic value as antique art pieces. My find had to be handed over to the authorities as treasure trove, but the generous allowance they gave me made an immense difference to the circumstances of my family and myself.

L.S.

*   *   *

Seventh Letter.

With reference to your articles regarding re-incarnation, I wish to place these facts on record which, in my opinion, are a proof of a former existence.

During my school days I developed a peculiar habit of gesturing with my hands, absolutely foreign to a British child, which brought a lot of ridicule on my head; later on I always felt a strong urge to bow—not the bow one would make to a lady in the old days, but again a strangely foreign one. In later years I endeavoured to suppress these actions but they still persist at odd times.

I now come to the year 1913. Up to this time I dreamt very little and any dreams I had were fragmentary. I dreamt I was in a Square of what appeared to be an old world town of foreign appearance, at the far end was a high scaffolding and, I remember, when I looked at this, I shuddered.

I had the same dream again twice, the three being spread over a period of five or six weeks. They were so vivid at the time that I could have described everything I saw minutely. In the mean time I and my mother attended a fete at which a fortune-teller of foreign extraction was present. My mother decided to have a crystal reading, the fortune teller towards the end described the scene of my dream exactly, and asked my mother did she recognise it. She could not, of course, as I had not told anyone of the dreams, fearing ridicule. The lady finished by saying that " a member of our household would travel in a foreign country, would pass through great dangers and eventually come safely home. My mother described what she had been told. I then related my dreams. We thought it all very strange, but just put it down to coincidence.

Then 1914, war. I eventually joined up and and landed in France in late September, 1915. We disembarked at Havre. As soon as I put my foot on the dock-side a feeling of horror came over me, which was soon overcome by the excitement of war, for in those days I was young and eager.

We moved on and our next stop was Amiens. When we came into the town, again I had the feeling of horror, but this time conveyed with familiarity. I had the feeling that it was only yesterday since I had been there, and to add to my amazement I was able to direct my Company Commander, as to direction, even naming streets, and the first which came to my mind was the Place Gambetta, a notorious place during the revolution.

I had the same worrying experience in a number of other places, all as familiar as my own City, until late in 1917 we arrived at a little town named Corbie a few miles out of

Amiens. Again the sense of familiarity, this time very pronounced. During the afternoon I strolled round exploring and eventually came to the proverbial square. Up to this point I had completely forgotten about my dream, but now it came back like a flash, for here was the Square of my dream, which showed in the crystal. I was standing in the same spot looking at the high structure in the background, which turned out to be a guillotine which was preserved as a relic. I now began to feel nervous regarding these strange happenings, and decided to tell my Company Commander, an old friend of the family, about my dreams etc. While directing him through Amiens, on our arrival, he jokingly said, " it must be your second time on earth," and now said this was positive proof.

Now my family history—my name is C———, pure French as my ancestor was a French noble smuggled out of France during the Revolution and landed in Ireland where he settled like a good many more refugees. My late father had a record of the family tree, but this is now missing.

H.E.C.

*   *   *

Eighth Letter.

Some years ago I visited North Cornwall for the first time. A friend and I were to stay at a farm situated high on the cliffs, about seven miles from Bude and two miles from the nearest village. Our hostess met us at the station with a car and decided to drive to the farm by the coast road so that we could enjoy the view.

Our rooms had been booked by post, I had never met our hostess before, yet, something about her was familiar, I was conscious of a feeling of aversion, even though she was niceness itself. Her eyes were peculiar, one being blue and the other hazel.

Up on the downs the road seemed familiar, and when our hostess stopped to point out a landmark, I surprised both her and myself by remarking, " Oh yes, and just beneath this spot is the entrance to the old smugglers' cave."

" The cave, well there is talk of a smugglers' cave just on this stretch of coast, but the entrance has been blocked for years," she replied. " I cannot remember it ever being open, and I was born here."

That night I sat at my bedroom window, gazing out upon the wild scenery and listening to the roar of the sea, when suddenly I saw a vision. Another house, old, grey, with tiny lattice windows, appeared where the lawn of the farm house was. I saw a young man dressed in jerkin and plumed hat sitting astride a beautiful horse, beneath a tree, holding in one hand the reins of another horse. I saw a glimmer of light in one of the windows, saw the man signal with his hat, saw a few minutes later, a small door open, and a beautiful girl carrying a bundle, creep out. I watched the man dismount, saw him lift the girl into her saddle, and then just as he was about to remount a window flew open. An old man wearing a night cap on his head looked out, levelled an old-fashioned blunderbuss on the window ledge and fired. I saw the girl fall from the horse.

Then it was myself who was lying on the ground by her side, her warm blood mingling with mine. The old man bent over me, his eyes glared down into mine, then all was black.

The next morning I related this experience. "Dreaming," scoffed my hostess, but the look of sheer hatred in her eyes startled me.

Her husband supplied the missing link. "You are re-living history, Miss," he said, "That dream of yours really happened in the wife's family one hundred and fifty years ago. One of her forebears was the squire of this place and lived in the manor house on this site. The old man had quarrelled with a neighbour who farmed up there in the hills. The son of his enemy fell in love with the old man's daughter, but he forbade the lovers to meet. They decided to elope, were in the act of doing this when the old man was aroused. He fired from the window, meaning to kill the young man, instead, he killed them both."

The strangest part of the story is that *I* was that young man, my hostess was possessed of odd coloured eyes, and so were the eyes of the old man who had a century and a half ago, knelt over my murdered body.

A.D.M.

* * *

Ninth Letter.

During the Great War I had an experience which has always seemed unexplainable and was at the time most startling.

Whilst serving in the 51st Sussex Regt. as a corporal, with the Army of Occupation on the Rhine, I was sent to the outpost line with a small party of men.

The village we reached early one morning and I was given a list of the houses where the men were to be billeted.

Without realising what I was doing I gave each the number of the house and the name of the street where he was to go, but what is more I gave each detailed instructions on how to get to their respective houses.

It was not until a remark made by one of the men to the effect that I must have been there before the War, that I realized what I had done.

Every little part of the village was even more familiar to me than the part of North London where I was born and had lived until the time of enlistment.

Certain of the older inhabitants also seemed to think they knew me, and I them, although this was an absolute impossibility.

A stream where we went to swim, and which was in places very dangerous, was so impressed on my mind that I named quite a number of dangers which even some of the peasants did not know.

I have had similar experiences but of a much milder nature in other parts of Germany.

It was one of the men who were with me that drew my attention to the letters in " *Pearson's Weekly* " and I know of at least one other available who would verify the facts.

L.B.K.

Tenth Letter.

Dear Miss Baronte,—I have had several experiences which have proved to me the truth of Re-incarnation, but I think this is the best one, as it convinced another person as well.

I was coming out of a large building and as there was rather a crowd, I happened to get stopped near to the door. I looked up, and met the eyes of a man who was standing a few yards away from me.

The walls of the room, and the crowd disappeared, I felt that time had rolled back, I was living in the past, and I knew that this man had been a friend of mine. Afterwards, when I did know him, and we compared notes, I found that the recognition had been mutual.

E.O.

* * *

Eleventh Letter.

A Recurring Dream.

Since childhood I have had a vivid dream after which I ache all over as though I really had been on a very long journey. I am in company with many more elderly women and we are compelled to travel far to appear before " His Majesty " who has commanded his women subjects to appear before him (women between 50 and 55 years of age) hoping he will find his mother among them.

We are driven forward like a herd of cattle, dressed in coarse garments girdled at the waist, and rough sandals on our feet. Our hair, curiously dark for our years, is thick and is cut in a long straight " bob."

We are weary, hot, and thirsty, but are not allowed to rest.

At last we come to a beautiful flat-roofed building, apparently built in marble, with gorgeous-plumed birds and cool fountains, and brilliant sunshine.

At the bottom of some wide steps a man is standing anxiously scanning the faces of the women. We are arranged to pass before him in twos.

He has an arresting lovely face although pale, and delicate looking, and wears a long flowing garment and has a black beard and hair and large dark eyes. His hand is outstretched as the women pass before him.

At last I stand face towards him and I recognise him as my son.

His face lights up as he says " At last. My mother " and I run to him and wake up bathed in perspiration.

In this life I had a son who was a helpless invalid for twenty-five years. As he grew older the likeness to the man in my dream was most remarkable.

Strange to say I have not had the dream since he died.

A.G.

FIFTH CHAPTER

THE AURA.

" CAN you see my aura? " is the question which more than two-thirds of my clients, who come to me for personal interviews, ask me. The next question is " Can I acquire occult vision so that I can see the aura? " I have to explain that occult vision is not required for the purpose of seeing the aura. What is required is perfected physical vision.

The aura is stored light. This light is stored in the body as phosphorous is stored in animal and vegetable matter. Electricity (nature's magnetism) will sometimes render phosphorescent matter which is not so naturally. Our chemists know that if we take a vacuum tube charged with the kathode ray into a dark room and place it inside a black cylinder, any form which comes between the cylinder and a nearby screen will be thrown on the screen. The light is entirely intercepted by the black cylinder, and yet it throws up the shadow. If a little flourescent matter is placed on the screen the light in the cylinder will cause it to glow. This is what happens when auras are seen. The electric ray which projects such things has met the eye which can vibrate with it.

Auras are caused by fluids in the body which generate light which takes onto itself certain colours. It is the health, not the spiritual attainment which can be judged by the aura.

The vibration which produces blue in an aura is usually missing with very nervous people. If I do not see it surrounding the person who interviews me, I suggest certain treatments having to do with the sympathetic or nervous system.

This system is energised by outside waves and not by the body. The body but furnishes substance called nerves into which outside energy flows. In the coming years our medical scientists will cease pouring medicine down our throats with the hope of curing our nerves. No disease of the nerves has ever been cured by internal treatment. Scientists will learn to speed up and to slow down the outside energy, and they will teach us how to become more or less susceptible to outside influences. Our bodies are barometers which vibrate to every change of atmosphere; but no medical man gives a thought to this any more than to tell us to be beware of chills and to guard against becoming overheated. The tremendous range of atmospheric affects between these two points is entirely ignored. Storms produce a great disturbance in our auras which shows that our contacts (of energy) are racing wildly or diminished.

The tesseract, or fourth-dimensional cube, was introduced to express in a clumsy way, the permeability of matter. We hear a lot about the fourth dimension, but nothing is said about the other dimensions which influence the body by waves which penetrate the fourth dimension and disturb our equilibrium. To vibrate with these currents we require a different body; one which uses as food substance that cannot decay. The only food which we eat at present which does not decay is honey. Honey may crystallize or dry, but these are forms of preservation. The ancient Egyptians and the Chinese knew the value of honey for restoring body-equilibrium. Dieticians tell us that it has the same value as sugar, but that it is better for us than sugar. They do not know that it is a form of energy. The holy men of India who allow their bodies to be buried in the earth for forty days, take honey as their last food before they start the fast which prepares them for the temporary burial. It is the first food they take after the ordeal. We have already learned to balance our foods to a certain extent. In the future we shall learn to eat less and to breathe more. When the air, as we call it (it is really a high vibration struggling in dense matter) can reach us in its pure form it will entirely nourish us. We cannot understand this at present because we can think only in terms of chewing, swallowing and digesting. Our digested food produces a slight form of energy. Think what it will mean when we consume bare energy—energy which cannot decay. It is a wave from this energy which puts our vegetation to sleep—and causes it to bloom again.

It is difficult for us to believe that a day will come when we shall no longer need our present vegetation for food. We shall become very practical. We shall learn to carry nothing on our backs which does not add to our advancement. Our form will change its appearance. Our watchwords are knowledge and elimination. We must learn to eliminate all the useless things which litter the world. Everything we need is stored in the greater energy. We must learn how to receive our gifts.

In the future there will be no aura. Human beings will have achieved perfect health. The fluids and gases which produce the aura will be diverted. The forms in the greater energy do not project colour. This is known to those who can extend their vision (heighten their senses to contact waves far stronger than any known to television).

The aura has nothing to do with the magnetic emanations which project from certain people. This emanation is generated by soul-power. It was said to extend from Buddha to the distance of four miles.

SIXTH CHAPTER

METALS AND HERBS.

NOT long ago a Chinese doctor came to see me to ask if I knew anything about the action of metals on the human body. He was treating illnesses with metals. This was a subject I had studied in India, when, with an Indian scientist, I discussed the analogies which metals present with living organisms.

I learned under the direction of the Indian scientist, that metals succumb to disease as animals do, and that they have definite periods of growth—that they possess intelligence, sensitiveness and nerves—that they change their forms as everything else in the universe does while retaining their fundamental characteristics.

The transmutation of metals was ridiculed for years until certain scientists actually saw one element change into another. They changed phosphorous, arsenic and antimony, the one into the other.

The doctor told me that he was treating several diseases with coral, and certain other diseases with gold. It is strange that so many people think of coral as a mineral. The doctor knew it was an animal product but he had classed it with his metals. Considering that he discussed the sex of coral it was rather amusing to hear him refer to it as belonging to his group of metals. In most corals, the colonies are either male or female. The ancient Indian healers who used coral in the treatment of disease chose coral from the female reefs. It was said to be more rapid in its cures than the male coral. The Chinese Doctor was of the same opinion. He chose the female coral and usually the deep red variety. He found that it produced energy in the blood and activity in the liver.

People who write to ask me what metal belongs to them, usually tell me that they feel better when wearing some special metal. This is because they vibrate with the metal they mention. Their rate of energy is the same as the rate which produces the metal. The energy which crystallizes and forms a mineral or metal is the same which flows into the body but the flesh transmutes the energy into action. Energy acts differently in different substances.

A man in America almost succeeded in making gold. His process consisted of certain chemical reactions produced by powerful vibratory waves combined with high pressure. He was not successful because he did not know how to arrange his substance for the attraction of the energy which crystallizes. It will not be so long, however, before the world will be able to make any metal it wishes. There will come a time when gold will amount to no more than dirt under our feet. The science we call chemistry (it repudiates its parent, alchemy) is the wedge which will pry open the secret of transmutation of energy. Chemistry proceeds on occult lines, but no scientist will admit this. The old chemical and atomic theories have capsized because they could not hold water. The present theories will capsize in the same way as they are too elaborate, too full of wasted energy.

The future will learn to use the almost unlimited power of radium. Many substances which to-day we think could not contain radium, will in the future, be found to contain it! We believe now that the substance known as radium assimilates some energy from space which causes it to admit light and heat. Radium is solidified vibration (energy). Some day we shall intercept this power before it crystallizes. Radium throws off its energy without losing its bulk. It revitalizes itself by using itself. In this it follows the first universal law—the law which awaits recognition. In various potency radium would fight all our battles. It would annihilate a continent in a moment or it would light and heat and do all the work of a continent.

The metals have their rate of intelligence and sensitiveness. They frequently succumb to disease. So far as growth is concerned, iron, copper, gold and silver mines have been worked years after they were abandoned as " worked out."

Everyone expresses analogy with some metal. The ancient Chaldeans believed that gold, because it was the metal of the sun, belonged to man. As in modern astrology, the sun represented the male. The Chaldeans said that silver was the moon's metal and that it belonged to women. The other heavenly bodies had their metals. Venus had copper, Saturn lead etc.

To treat diseases with metals the doctor using the metals should be sure that the patient and the metal are on the same rate of vibration—this is especially true if the metals are to be taken internally.

There are records in Italian books of the middle ages, of people being cured of diseases by being surrounded with certain woods. There is the story of an Italian Countess—I do not recall her name—who was relieved of violent pain by having her bed strewn with ilex branches. I knew a Chinese Mandarin who slept with willow twigs under his head to ward off attacks of nose-bleed from which he suffered.

In India it is a common thing to burn saffron in a house which is said to be unlucky. The saffron overcomes the "bad luck." Rheumatism is frequently treated in India with the sap of the sacred fig tree. I have known several cures to be made with this sap. Cancer, in its early stages, has been cured with mistletoe. There is a hospital in Switzerland where cancer is now being treated with mistletoe. It is said that cures have been made in this institution. Occultists know that the vibration which produces the parasite known as cancer produces the parasite known as mistletoe.

Everything in the universe has some sort of consciousness, although it has many divisions and subdivisions. Regardless of how consciousness may manifest in human beings, plants or minerals, it comes from the same source—energy. When consciousness flows into the human brain it is conditioned by the will, and by limitations. Personality is a condition of the brain and of the will and not of the fundamental consciousness.

To the occultist, conscious matter emits a blue ray.

Unconscious matter (matter not animated by an ego) cannot emit this ray, because this ray is produced by the vibrations of an ego. The state of unconsciousness is caused by the withdrawal of this ray. A corpse or a person under the influence of ether cannot emit this ray. I look for this ray (clairvoyantly) when trying to help my clients. If it is very evident, the brain is responding to the higher energy as it should, and the will is controlling the sympathetic or nervous system.

To find the metal or plant which is in harmony with the personality, one must study the rate of energy expressed by the brain and by the *so called* inanimate objects.

I do not wish to go on record as having tried to help anyone by recommending the internal use of certain minerals and metals. I realise that we have an analogy with the metals because we have evolved through the minerals and the plants to the animal condition—but I have never suggested the use of them. I have mentioned to certain people the analogy of plants with the human organism but this is as far as I have gone, for herbalism should be a life study, and my work does not embrace it. I constantly have to inform my clients that my subject is re-incarnation and the reconstruction of the previous existence. By reconstructing the past I can throw some light on the present problems, and I hope in this way to be of some service to my fellow beings.

A
FEW LETTERS
OF APPRECIATION

Dear Madam,—I am in receipt of your incarnascope and the absolute accuracy of this man's characteristics is nothing short of marvellous.

E.P.

Business occasionally takes me to Bournemouth. If I am there long enough on my visit, I go to Christchurch Priory. The old Priory Church and the meadows behind, on the banks of the Avon, seemed strangely familiar, even on my first visit. I can visualise the old monks doing the wonderful under-cut stone carving.

I seem to have a memory of living in a monastery in a previous incarnation; of associating with the monks very closely, though not being quite one of them. The time seems rather before the dissolution of the monasteries.

An incarnation reading by Gervée Baronte gave my previous existence as 428 years ago—which brings us back to the period to which my memory seems to go and, she tells me, I was a lay preacher.

J.A.P.

A few weeks ago I happened to visit a cinema here in Carlisle. There was an Egyptian picture which appealed to me. It seemed to be the very place (as I sat and visualised) where I had a previous life and had lived before.

Many a time I thought about it and still to-day it seems to linger in my memory.

Although many times the film companies can fake a scene, this one was sure a shot from Egypt.

Also, when I made enquiries about my re-incarnation, Miss Baronte gave me this one:—

Occupation : Saite scribe (writer).
Place of previous Existence : Egypt.

and this must be true as I have taken for one of my hobbies from my last life—writing.

E.T.

In 1913 when managing ——— Hotel, London, a young officer who had studied re-incarnation, suddenly thought he recognised me as being his enemy a long time ago in Egypt. Going down Wardour Street he bought a knife and the next day ran amok. Flourishing the knife, he was going to kill me because I had been his enemy in a previous life. He was arrested. There was a trial. From the dock the prisoner still threatened, and quoted Tennyson.

About a year later I had a reading from Gervée Baronte and found that I had been in Egypt in 200 B.C. in a previous life and had done just what this man had accused me of doing.

C.R.

Dear Madam,—May I say "Thank you" for your unconscious collaboration in something I have been trying to do? You sent a re-incarnation chart to a friend, marked with the lesson to be learned "Restraint." That same day she had a letter from me saying: "Take a reef in, old thing; if you don't, something will heel over " She was so struck by the coincidence that she has just sent her chart on to me.

There is not the faintest doubt despite her Swedish-Irish ancestry, of her Indian past. Walk, general appearance, tastes and tendencies. During July of last year the lounge of this house was filled with Indians, mainly women, and Peggy Moran plus sari and caste mark would have passed unnoticed among them. Yet all her very real troubles result entirely from that lack of restraint, and there is another crash coming unless the coincidence of our joint remarks impresses her sufficiently. She is a sort of protegée of mine, handed over by my doctor because I am " probably the sanest woman on earth," so you will realize my anxiety and real gratitude for the coincidence.

F.E.C.

I have always been intensely interested in anything connected with France and the French people.

One of my favourite subjects at school was history and I invariably found myself taking an abnormal interest in any period when the English were involved either in a friendly or antagonistic manner with the French.

Historical French novels also fascinate me and I have revelled in any film or play depicting French scenes of any period. I felt so much in sympathy with the people and experienced an unaccountable sense of friendliness and knowledge of their ways.

This used to puzzle me very much for my family is entirely English. I have never been to France, and I have met very few French people.

Therefore when I received my reading from Gervée Baronte some short time ago, and learned that my previous incarnation was in France during the reign of Louis XIII, many of the things which had so greatly mystified me were explained.

(signed) " *Axel.*"

Dear Madam,—Last summer I wrote you, as I was interested in Re-incarnation and was curious to know what country you would say I lived in, in my last incarnation. I was not at all surprised when you replied Egypt.

When I lived near the British Museum I often used to go in, and always made for the Egyptian room at once. Then I thought very little about re-incarnation. The mummies had a great fascination for me. I suppose it would be possible to be looking at one's own mummy. Also, I do so dislike being buried under the ground. I don't want to die, but I am not afraid, if only my body could be kept as the mummies. I have had this feeling ever since I can remember. When I tell people they think me so queer.

I have always wanted to visit Egypt, but of course many people do. Perhaps I get my extraordinary love of cats, too, from my past life.

I look forward every week to " *Pearson's* " because of your articles. I find the symbols very true with regard to all the people so far, and look forward to some more.

Yours truly,

E.M.B.

ORDER FROM YOUR FAVORITE BOOKSELLER OR CALL FOR OUR FREE CATALOG

Babylonian Influence on the Bible and Popular Beliefs: A Comparative Study of Genesis 1.2, by A. Smythe Palmer. ISBN 1-58509-000-X • 124 pages • 6 x 9 • trade paper • $12.95

Biography of Satan: Exposing the Origins of the Devil, by Kersey Graves. ISBN 1-885395-11-6 • 168 pages • 5 1/2 x 8 1/2 • trade paper • $13.95

The Malleus Maleficarum: The Notorious Handbook Once Used to Condemn and Punish "Witches", by Heinrich Kramer and James Sprenger. ISBN 1-58509-098-0 • 332 pages • 6 x 9 • trade paper • $25.95

Crux Ansata: An Indictment of the Roman Catholic Church, by H. G. Wells. ISBN 1-58509-210-X • 160 pages • 6 x 9 • trade paper • $14.95

Emanuel Swedenborg: The Spiritual Columbus, by U.S.E. (William Spear). ISBN 1-58509-096-4 • 208 pages • 6 x 9 • trade paper • $17.95

Dragons and Dragon Lore, by Ernest Ingersoll. ISBN 1-58509-021-2 • 228 pages • 6 x 9 • trade paper • illustrated • $17.95

The Vision of God, by Nicholas of Cusa. ISBN 1-58509-004-2 • 160 pages • 5 x 8 • trade paper • $13.95

The Historical Jesus and the Mythical Christ: Separating Fact From Fiction, by Gerald Massey. ISBN 1-58509-073-5 • 244 pages • 6 x 9 • trade paper • $18.95

Gog and Magog: The Giants in Guildhall; Their Real and Legendary History, with an Account of Other Giants at Home and Abroad, by F.W. Fairholt. ISBN 1-58509-084-0 • 172 pages • 6 x 9 • trade paper • $16.95

The Origin and Evolution of Religion, by Albert Churchward. ISBN 1-58509-078-6 • 504 pages • 6 x 9 • trade paper • $39.95

The Origin of Biblical Traditions, by Albert T. Clay. ISBN 1-58509-065-4 • 220 pages • 5 1/2 x 8 1/2 • trade paper • $17.95

Aryan Sun Myths, by Sarah Elizabeth Titcomb, Introduction by Charles Morris. ISBN 1-58509-069-7 • 192 pages • 6 x 9 • trade paper • $15.95

The Social Record of Christianity, by Joseph McCabe. Includes **The Lies and Fallacies of the Encyclopedia Britannica**, ISBN 1-58509-215-0 • 204 pages • 6 x 9 • trade paper • $17.95

The History of the Christian Religion and Church During the First Three Centuries, by Dr. Augustus Neander. ISBN 1-58509-077-8 • 112 pages • 6 x 9 • trade paper • $12.95

Ancient Symbol Worship: Influence of the Phallic Idea in the Religions of Antiquity, by Hodder M. Westropp and C. Staniland Wake. ISBN 1-58509-048-4 • 120 pages • 6 x 9 • trade paper • illustrated • $12.95

The Gnosis: Or Ancient Wisdom in the Christian Scriptures, by William Kingsland. ISBN 1-58509-047-6 • 232 pages • 6 x 9 • trade paper • $18.95

The Evolution of the Idea of God: An Inquiry into the Origin of Religions, by Grant Allen. ISBN 1-58509-074-3 • 160 pages • 6 x 9 • trade paper • $14.95

Sun Lore of All Ages: A Survey of Solar Mythology, Folklore, Customs, Worship, Festivals, and Superstition, by William Tyler Olcott. ISBN 1-58509-044-1 • 316 pages • 6 x 9 • trade paper • $24.95

Nature Worship: An Account of Phallic Faiths and Practices Ancient and Modern, by the Author of Phallicism with an Introduction by Tedd St. Rain. ISBN 1-58509-049-2 • 112 pages • 6 x 9 • trade paper • illustrated • $12.95

Life and Religion, by Max Muller. ISBN 1-885395-10-8 • 237 pages • 5 1/2 x 8 1/2 • trade paper • $14.95

Jesus: God, Man, or Myth? An Examination of the Evidence, by Herbert Cutner. ISBN 1-58509-072-7 • 304 pages • 6 x 9 • trade paper • $23.95

Pagan and Christian Creeds: Their Origin and Meaning, by Edward Carpenter. ISBN 1-58509-024-7 • 316 pages • 5 1/2 x 8 1/2 • trade paper • $24.95

The Christ Myth: A Study, by Elizabeth Evans. ISBN 1-58509-037-9 • 136 pages • 6 x 9 • trade paper • $13.95

Popery: Foe of the Church and the Republic, by Joseph F. Van Dyke. ISBN 1-58509-058-1 • 336 pages • 6 x 9 • trade paper • illustrated • $25.95

Career of Religious Ideas, by Hudson Tuttle. ISBN 1-58509-066-2 • 172 pages • 5 x 8 • trade paper • $15.95

Buddhist Suttas: Major Scriptural Writings from Early Buddhism, by T.W. Rhys Davids. ISBN 1-58509-079-4 • 376 pages • 6 x 9 • trade paper • $27.95

Early Buddhism, by T. W. Rhys Davids. Includes **Buddhist Ethics: The Way to Salvation?**, by Paul Tice. ISBN 1-58509-076-X • 112 pages • 6 x 9 • trade paper • $12.95

The Fountain-Head of Religion: A Comparative Study of the Principal Religions of the World and a Manifestation of their Common Origin from the Vedas, by Ganga Prasad. ISBN 1-58509-054-9 • 276 pages • 6 x 9 • trade paper • $22.95

India: What Can It Teach Us?, by Max Muller. ISBN 1-58509-064-6 • 284 pages • 5 1/2 x 8 1/2 • trade paper • $22.95

Matrix of Power: How the World has Been Controlled by Powerful People Without Your Knowledge, by Jordan Maxwell. ISBN 1-58509-120-0 • 104 pages • 6 x 9 • trade paper • $12.95

Cyberculture Counterconspiracy: A Steamshovel Web Reader, Volume One, edited by Kenn Thomas. ISBN 1-58509-125-1 • 180 pages • 6 x 9 • trade paper • illustrated • $16.95

Cyberculture Counterconspiracy: A Steamshovel Web Reader, Volume Two, edited by Kenn Thomas. ISBN 1-58509-126-X • 132 pages • 6 x 9 • trade paper • illustrated • $13.95

Oklahoma City Bombing: The Suppressed Truth, by Jon Rappoport. ISBN 1-885395-22-1 • 112 pages • 5 1/2 x 8 1/2 • trade paper • $12.95

The Protocols of the Learned Elders of Zion, by Victor Marsden. ISBN 1-58509-015-8 • 312 pages • 6 x 9 • trade paper • $24.95

Secret Societies and Subversive Movements, by Nesta H. Webster. ISBN 1-58509-092-1 • 432 pages • 6 x 9 • trade paper • $29.95

The Secret Doctrine of the Rosicrucians, by Magus Incognito. ISBN 1-58509-091-3 • 256 pages • 6 x 9 • trade paper • $20.95

The Origin and Evolution of Freemasonry: Connected with the Origin and Evolution of the Human Race, by Albert Churchward. ISBN 1-58509-029-8 • 240 pages • 6 x 9 • trade paper • $18.95

The Lost Key: An Explanation and Application of Masonic Symbols, by Prentiss Tucker. ISBN 1-58509-050-6 • 192 pages • 6 x 9 • trade paper • illustrated • $15.95

The Character, Claims, and Practical Workings of Freemasonry, by Rev. C.G. Finney. ISBN 1-58509-094-8 • 288 pages • 6 x 9 • trade paper • $22.95

The Secret World Government or "The Hidden Hand": The Unrevealed in History, by Maj.-Gen. Count Cherep-Spiridovich. ISBN 1-58509-093-X • 270 pages • 6 x 9 • trade paper • $21.95

The Magus, Book One: A Complete System of Occult Philosophy, by Francis Barrett. ISBN 1-58509-031-X • 200 pages • 6 x 9 • trade paper • illustrated • $16.95

The Magus, Book Two: A Complete System of Occult Philosophy, by Francis Barrett. ISBN 1-58509-032-8 • 220 pages • 6 x 9 • trade paper • illustrated • $17.95

The Magus, Book One and Two: A Complete System of Occult Philosophy, by Francis Barrett. ISBN 1-58509-033-6 • 420 pages • 6 x 9 • trade paper • illustrated • $34.90

The Key of Solomon The King, by S. Liddell MacGregor Mathers. ISBN 1-58509-022-0 • 152 pages • 6 x 9 • trade paper • illustrated • $12.95

Magic and Mystery in Tibet, by Alexandra David-Neel. ISBN 1-58509-097-2 • 352 pages • 6 x 9 • trade paper • $26.95

The Comte de St. Germain, by I. Cooper Oakley. ISBN 1-58509-068-9 • 280 pages • 6 x 9 • trade paper • illustrated • $22.95

Alchemy Rediscovered and Restored, by A. Cockren. ISBN 1-58509-028-X • 156 pages • 5 1/2 x 8 1/2 • trade paper • $13.95

The 6th and 7th Books of Moses, with an Introduction by Paul Tice. ISBN 1-58509-045-X • 188 pages • 6 x 9 • trade paper • illustrated • $16.95

ORDER FROM YOUR FAVORITE BOOKSELLER OR CALL FOR OUR FREE CATALOG

Of Heaven and Earth: Essays Presented at the First Sitchin Studies Day, edited by Zecharia Sitchin. ISBN 1-885395-17-5 • 164 pages • 5 1/2 x 8 1/2 • trade paper • illustrated • $14.95

God Games: What Do You Do Forever?, by Neil Freer. ISBN 1-885395-39-6 • 312 pages • 6 x 9 • trade paper • $19.95

Space Travelers and the Genesis of the Human Form: Evidence of Intelligent Contact in the Solar System, by Joan d'Arc. ISBN 1-58509-127-8 • 208 pages • 6 x 9 • trade paper • illustrated • $18.95

Humanity's Extraterrestrial Origins: ET Influences on Humankind's Biological and Cultural Evolution, by Dr. Arthur David Horn with Lynette Mallory-Horn. ISBN 3-931652-31-9 • 373 pages • 6 x 9 • trade paper • $17.00

Past Shock: The Origin of Religion and Its Impact on the Human Soul, by Jack Barranger. ISBN 1-885395-08-6 • 126 pages • 6 x 9 • trade paper • illustrated • $12.95

Flying Serpents and Dragons: The Story of Mankind's Reptilian Past, by R.A. Boulay. ISBN 1-885395-38-8 • 276 pages • 6 x 9 • trade paper • illustrated • $19.95

Triumph of the Human Spirit: The Greatest Achievements of the Human Soul and How Its Power Can Change Your Life, by Paul Tice. ISBN 1-885395-57-4 • 295 pages • 6 x 9 • trade paper • illustrated • $19.95

Mysteries Explored: The Search for Human Origins, UFOs, and Religious Beginnings, by Jack Barranger and Paul Tice. ISBN 1-58509-101-4 • 104 pages • 6 x 9 • trade paper • $12.95

Mushrooms and Mankind: The Impact of Mushrooms on Human Consciousness and Religion, by James Arthur. ISBN 1-58509-151-0 • 103 pages • 6 x 9 • trade paper • $12.95

Vril or Vital Magnetism, with an Introduction by Paul Tice. ISBN 1-58509-030-1 • 124 pages • 5 1/2 x 8 1/2 • trade paper • $12.95

The Odic Force: Letters on Od and Magnetism, by Karl von Reichenbach. ISBN 1-58509-001-8 • 192 pages • 6 x 9 • trade paper • $15.95

The New Revelation: The Coming of a New Spiritual Paradigm, by Arthur Conan Doyle. ISBN 1-58509-220-7 • 124 pages • 6 x 9 • trade paper • $12.95

The Astral World: Its Scenes, Dwellers, and Phenomena, by Swami Panchadasi. ISBN 1-58509-071-9 • 104 pages • 6 x 9 • trade paper • $11.95

Reason and Belief: The Impact of Scientific Discovery on Religious and Spiritual Faith, by Sir Oliver Lodge. ISBN 1-58509-226-6 • 180 pages • 6 x 9 • trade paper • $17.95

William Blake: A Biography, by Basil De Selincourt. ISBN 1-58509-225-8 • 384 pages • 6 x 9 • trade paper • $28.95

The Divine Pymander: And Other Writings of Hermes Trismegistus, translated by John D. Chambers. ISBN 1-58509-046-2 • 196 pages • 6 x 9 • trade paper • $16.95

Theosophy and The Secret Doctrine, by Harriet L. Henderson. Includes *H.P. Blavatsky: An Outline of Her Life,* by Herbert Whyte, ISBN 1-58509-075-1 • 132 pages • 6 x 9 • trade paper • $13.95

The Light of Egypt, Volume One: The Science of the Soul and the Stars, by Thomas H. Burgoyne. ISBN 1-58509-051-4 • 320 pages • 6 x 9 • trade paper • illustrated • $24.95

The Light of Egypt, Volume Two: The Science of the Soul and the Stars, by Thomas H. Burgoyne. ISBN 1-58509-052-2 • 224 pages • 6 x 9 • trade paper • illustrated • $17.95

The Jumping Frog and 18 Other Stories: 19 Unforgettable Mark Twain Stories, by Mark Twain. ISBN 1-58509-200-2 • 128 pages • 6 x 9 • trade paper • $12.95

The Devil's Dictionary: A Guidebook for Cynics, by Ambrose Bierce. ISBN 1-58509-016-6 • 144 pages • 6 x 9 • trade paper • $12.95

The Smoky God: Or The Voyage to the Inner World, by Willis George Emerson. ISBN 1-58509-067-0 • 184 pages • 6 x 9 • trade paper • illustrated • $15.95

A Short History of the World, by H.G. Wells. ISBN 1-58509-211-8 • 320 pages • 6 x 9 • trade paper • $24.95

The Voyages and Discoveries of the Companions of Columbus, by Washington Irving. ISBN 1-58509-500-1 • 352 pages • 6 x 9 • hard cover • $39.95

History of Baalbek, by Michel Alouf. ISBN 1-58509-063-8 • 196 pages • 5 x 8 • trade paper • illustrated • $15.95

Ancient Egyptian Masonry: The Building Craft, by Sommers Clarke and R. Engelback. ISBN 1-58509-059-X • 350 pages • 6 x 9 • trade paper • illustrated • $26.95

That Old Time Religion: The Story of Religious Foundations, by Jordan Maxwell and Paul Tice. ISBN 1-58509-100-6 • 103 pages • 6 x 9 • trade paper • $12.95

The Book of Enoch: A Work of Visionary Revelation and Prophecy, Revealing Divine Secrets and Fantastic Information about Creation, Salvation, Heaven and Hell, translated by R. H. Charles. ISBN 1-58509-019-0 • 152 pages • 5 1/2 x 8 1/2 • trade paper • $13.95

The Book of Enoch: Translated from the Editor's Ethiopic Text and Edited with an Enlarged Introduction, Notes and Indexes, Together with a Reprint of the Greek Fragments, edited by R. H. Charles. ISBN 1-58509-080-8 • 448 pages • 6 x 9 • trade paper • $34.95

The Book of the Secrets of Enoch, translated from the Slavonic by W. R. Morfill, Edited, with Introduction and Notes by R. H. Charles. ISBN 1-58509-020-4 • 148 pages • 5 1/2 x 8 1/2 • trade paper • $13.95

Enuma Elish: The Seven Tablets of Creation, Volume One, by L. W. King. ISBN 1-58509-041-7 • 236 pages • 6 x 9 • trade paper • illustrated • $18.95

Enuma Elish: The Seven Tablets of Creation, Volume Two, by L. W. King. ISBN 1-58509-042-5 • 260 pages • 6 x 9 • trade paper • illustrated • $19.95

Enuma Elish, Volumes One and Two: The Seven Tablets of Creation, by L. W. King. Two volumes from above bound as one. ISBN 1-58509-043-3 • 496 pages • 6 x 9 • trade paper • illustrated • $38.90

The Archko Volume: Documents that Claim Proof to the Life, Death, and Resurrection of Christ, by Drs. McIntosh and Twyman. ISBN 1-58509-082-4 • 248 pages • 6 x 9 • trade paper • $20.95

The Lost Language of Symbolism: An Inquiry into the Origin of Certain Letters, Words, Names, Fairy-Tales, Folklore, and Mythologies, by Harold Bayley. ISBN 1-58509-070-0 • 384 pages • 6 x 9 • trade paper • $27.95

The Book of Jasher: A Suppressed Book that was Removed from the Bible, Referred to in Joshua and Second Samuel, translated by Albinus Alcuin (800 AD). ISBN 1-58509-081-6 • 304 pages • 6 x 9 • trade paper • $24.95

The Bible's Most Embarrassing Moments, with an Introduction by Paul Tice. ISBN 1-58509-025-5 • 172 pages • 5 x 8 • trade paper • $14.95

History of the Cross: The Pagan Origin and Idolatrous Adoption and Worship of the Image, by Henry Dana Ward. ISBN 1-58509-056-5 • 104 pages • 6 x 9 • trade paper • illustrated • $11.95

Was Jesus Influenced by Buddhism? A Comparative Study of the Lives and Thoughts of Gautama and Jesus, by Dwight Goddard. ISBN 1-58509-027-1 • 252 pages • 6 x 9 • trade paper • $19.95

History of the Christian Religion to the Year Two Hundred, by Charles B. Waite. ISBN 1-885395-15-9 • 556 pages • 6 x 9 • hard cover • $25.00

Symbols, Sex, and the Stars, by Ernest Busenbark. ISBN 1-885395-19-1 • 396 pages • 5 1/2 x 8 1/2 • trade paper • $22.95

History of the First Council of Nice: A World's Christian Convention, A.D. 325, by Dean Dudley. ISBN 1-58509-023-9 • 132 pages • 5 1/2 x 8 1/2 • trade paper • $12.95

The World's Sixteen Crucified Saviors, by Kersey Graves. ISBN 1-58509-018-2 • 436 pages • 5 1/2 x 8 1/2 • trade paper • $29.95

www.ingramcontent.com/pod-product-compliance
Lightning Source LLC
Chambersburg PA
CBHW020020050426
42450CB00005B/565